The Red Army Stumbles

Perry Pierik

The Red Army Stumbles

Russian campaign
1941

Aspekt Publishers

The Red Army Stumbles

© Perry Pierik
© 2023 Aspekt Publishers
Amersfoortsestraat 27, 3769 AD Soesterberg, the Netherlands
info@uitgeverijaspekt.nl-http://www.uitgeverijaspekt.nl

Translated by: Ellen van den Broek
Edited by: Isabel Oomen
Cover: Mark Heuveling
Interlining: Maarten Bakker

ISBN: 9789461538598
NUR: 680

All rights reserved. No part of these pages, either text or image may be used for any purpose other than personal use. Therefore, reproduction, modification, storage in a retrieval system or retransmission, in any form or by any means, electronic, mechanical or

Table of Content

Introduction — 9

Stalin is Surprised. Moscow Considered Nazi-Germany to be the 'Weakest Link' in the War against France — 17

Russia's Field Army is Stationed Far to the West in the Field — 23

The Clash of Titans — 29

The Catastrophic Consequences of Moscow's Offensive Strategy — 33

Millions of Red Army Soldiers Perish During the 'Kessel' Campaigns — 37

Economic Warfare: the Campaign for 'Lebensraum' — 45

From Ostwall to Generalplan Ost — 51

Migration — 57

A Breadbasket in Western Ukraine — 61

Industry in Eastern Ukraine	65
The Soviet Union, a Logistical Nightmare, Railway Problems Severely Underestimated	69
The Three Regiments of the 'Grosstransportraum'	73
A War for Oil, waged 'Without Fuel'	79
The German War Industry was not suited for Mass Production	83
Problems among the Armed Forces: the Missing Feldhaubitze 18	85
Hitler Believed the PzKw III Tank to be a 'Failure'	87
A Large Junkyard	95
Changing Routes, the German High Command Hesitatest	99
Foolhardiness until the End; the Small-Scale Attack on Moscow by the 4th army and the Pz.gruppe 4	103

Operation 'Taifun' Fails	107
'Barbarossa', Beria, Purging and Terror	113
The Third Reich was Skilled with Conquests, but Bad with Consolidation	119
The Stubborn, Tough Russian Soldier	125
Afterword	129
Annex 1	131
Literature	133

Stalin is Surprised
Moscow Considered Nazi-Germany to be the 'Weakest Link' in the War against France

This book primarily discusses the showdown between Berlin and Moscow; it will not discuss the more metaphysical and ideological foundations of the German attack on the Soviet Union. One of the things that has engaged historians for a long time is the question of what the enormous accumulation of Soviet troops were doing in the western part of Russia, the Ukraine, and in occupied Poland. Nowhere else did the German 'Blitzkrieg' cause as much losses as in these areas. Entire armies were cut off from the hinterland by the 'Wehrmacht' and destroyed, which resulted in hundreds of thousands of deaths and millions of prisoners of war. These past decades many historians have emphasized that the Soviet armies were positioned this far to the west so Stalin could invade Western-Europe at any time. Some even stated that operation 'Barbarossa', the German attack on the Soviet-Union, was a preventive

Above: The German occupation of the Soviet Union had many consequences for the population
Below: Soviet infantry 23 June, 1941, the war is one day old

Above: T34 Tank
Below: A Russian Heavy T28 Tank

offensive. Both statements are probably wrong, starting with Hitler's attack on Russia. This attack was not the result of a chain of subsequent events, however, it also did not 'just' happen. In his earliest ideological works, Hitler already spoke of his desire for 'Lebensraum', and he repeated these words often. The actual conceptionalizing of that idea and the creation of plans did commence relatively late, and was highly motivated by practical considerations. With or without Stalin's offensive plans, Hitler would have chosen the offensive.

The notion that Stalin had intended to attack during the summer of 1941 is also very unlikely. However, it is a

BT 7 Tank of the Red Army

fact that the Kremlin had chosen for an invading strategy, and that the armies had offensively been drawn up, which fits with the Soviet military doctrine. Stalin had thought and hoped that Germany would weaken itself during the war against France and England, after which Moscow could easily take control. After a victory against Germany – which no-one expected! – Stalin assumed a strong communist revolution would sweep occupied Europe, which would benefit the world revolution. The occupation of Europe fragmented the German strength and Stalin believed that time was on his side.

Despite the surprise of the quick German victory, Moscow still felt that the gods of war were on their side. Stalin believed that Germany would not repeat the mistake of 1914-1918 by opening a second front. As a result, the focus in Moscow was strongly aimed at detecting any possible peace talks between London and Berlin. This turned out to be a serious misjudgement. Germany, which Stalin had said was the weakest link during a secret conference on 19-08-1939, had successfully rid itself of the French threat and aimed for the Soviet Union, even without peace. Stalin had literally been blown away because of this enormous gamble made by Hitler. The moment Nazi-Germany invaded Russia, a large part of the Soviet forces was stationed in the western part of the Soviet Union, and in the East of Poland. It concerned 300 divisions, 23.000 tanks and thousands of planes. Hitler invaded with a mere 149 divisions and 3.580 tanks, not included the several reserves and allies, which both parties brought to the front later on. Germany had painfully surprised Moscow.

Introduction

When reports surfaced concerning the Soviet losses at the battle around Vyazma-Bryansk (more than 600.000 losses), press agent Otto Dietrich stated that Nazi-Germany had won the war. Even Hitler boasted in several documents that Stalin had been defeated. He considered the war against Russia as part of something bigger. In the 'Generalplan Ost' the Russian loot had already been distributed, and the general public was left behind to live lives as slaves or die of starvation. Afterwards, Nazi-Germany would force Europe to 'hold its breath' as one was now ready to commence the war of the continents. Hitler was playing a game of geopolitics on the largest imaginable chessboard. And yes, the Red Army did stumble, after it had lost at Kiev, and among others at 'Kessel' hundreds of thousands, yes even millions of soldiers. The Soviet army had offensively been positioned at the western border and paid a terrible price for

The German invasion surprised Joseph Stalin

General Georgy Zjoekov, defender of Leningrad and Moscow

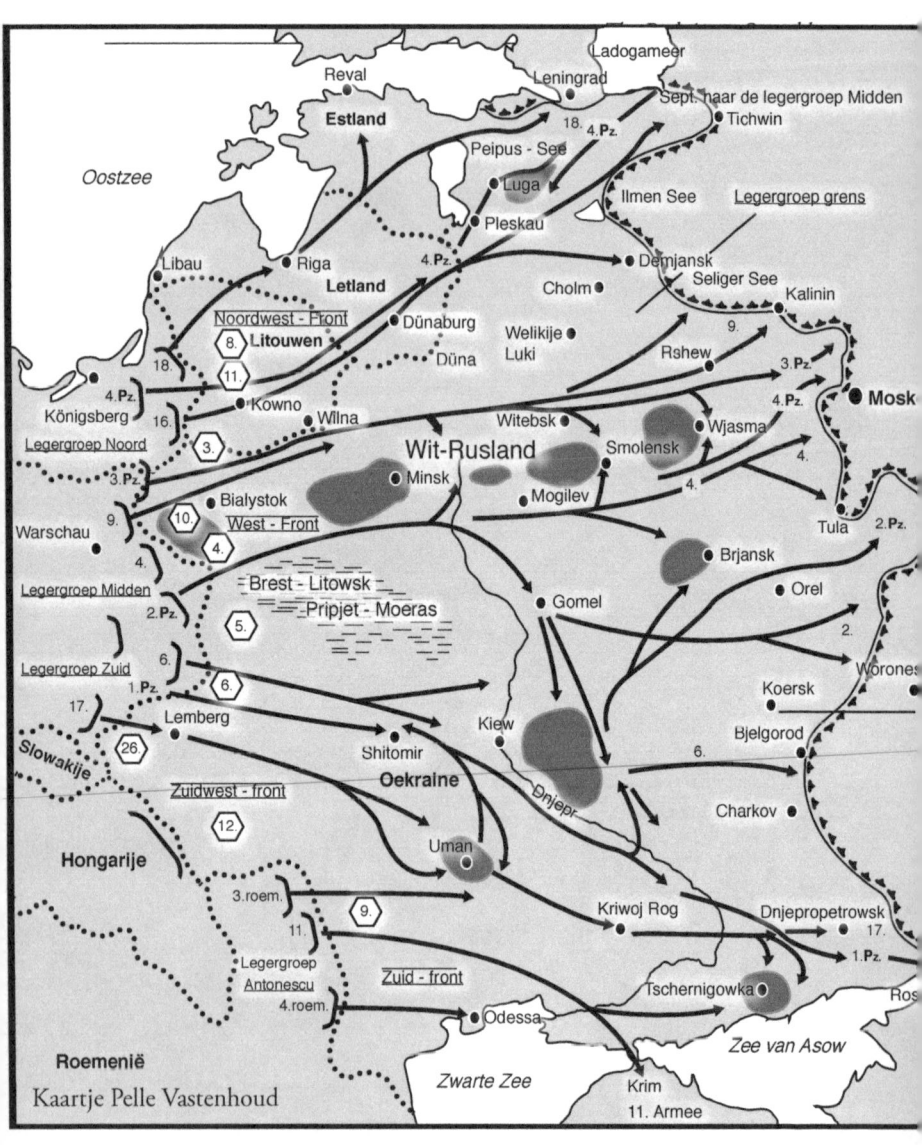

Operation Barbarossa 1941 and the encirclement
battles against the Red Army

Otto Dietrich spoke, after the battle at Vyazma, of the destruction of the Red Army

Above: Tank General Heinz Guderian
Below: Hitler and General Von Kluge

Introduction

it in June of 1941. However, as much as the Red Army did stumble, it never fell. During the terrible attacks at the border a lot of German attackers lost their lives, in addition to material, and strength. They had severely underestimated the logistical and economic problems of the campaign. Even certain standardized matters weren't taken care of; the problems with the Russian tracks, for instance, the extradition of heavy tanks before the start of 'Barbarossa', and the lack of standard weaponry, such as heavy howitzers in all infantry divisions. In addition, one had to consider the Soviet soldier: tough and stubborn, and their management that did not shy away from maintaining the most appalling terror. Amidst the chaos

Heinrich Himmler, head of the SS, visits a prisoners camp filled with Russian prisoners

of the German management, with shortages and terror, the sympathy of part of the population of the Ukraine turned into distrust and disappointment. When operation 'Taifun' stranded before Moscow this was not so much the result of the great Russian resistance. In fact, Zjoekov had relatively little troops lined up before the 186 miles long front line before the capital. However, because he focused on the right matters – the few roads – the Germans ultimately retreated, because their numbers were too small, and they arrived at the gates of Moscow too late. A wandering policy and the continuous change in priorities was to blame at this point. As we will see the doubt concerning the purpose and design of operation 'Barbarossa' started just days after the raid. What remained constant was the German boldness, which allowed the stumbling Red Army to regroup and helped them survive the winter of 1941-1942.

Dr. Perry Pierik

Russia's Field Army is Stationed Far to the West in the Field

Operation 'Barbarossa' is a history of mutual underestimation. The moment Nazi-Germany invaded it met a far stronger opponent than it had ever faced. The Soviet army had spared no expense to establish itself as a modern army. The Soviet strategists had kept an eye on the German military experiences. They did not shy away from changing their entire tactics and strategy as a result of what their research had shown them. Primarily, the Red Army had focused on creating tank brigades with regards to mobile warfare. The so-called tank corps from 1938 was comprised of two brigades: a light and a heavy brigade, equipped with tanks of types BT (light) and T-28 and T-35 (heavy). However, the experiences during the 'Blitzkrieg' taught them that they had to operate with a larger formation, and that the coherence of the motorized units was essen-

The German Army met heavy Soviet tanks: pictured here are two KV-1 tanks

tial. In Finland one had only experimented with one panzer unit, which, unfortunately, turned out to be a disaster due to the wooded front. The Spanish civil war had shown the tanks' vulnerability in acting against the artillery, but also in relation to the infantry in the event the tanks were forced to operate on their own. Even the Polish campaign did not offer spectacular results. The Soviets deployed two large panzer units, however, general Eremenko believed that 'the cavalry left more of an impression than the tanks'. The consequent conclusion was that they could learn from the German forces, which operated in groups. As a result, the so-called 'mechanized forces' were introduced to the army. On 2 June, the Red army had 20 armies at its disposal, of which 6 were stationed in Asia. These armies were comprised of 62 infantry corpses. A Soviet infantry corps was built as such:

Soviet Infantry Corps 1941

3 infantry divisions (1 division was comprised of 14.483 men)
2 artillery regiments
And three supporting battalions
In total: 50.000 men and 966 pieces of artillery and mortars

In total these corpses had 179 infantry divisions and 19 mountain divisions at its disposal. The panzer units and motorized infantry were placed in the mechanized corpses, which were essential due to the offensive attitude of the Red Army in the border areas. Overall, it concerned 29 corpses, consisting of 58 tank divisions and 29 motorized divisions, in addition to 3 tank divisions in other units. The mechanized corps was designed as such in 1941:

Soviet Mechanized Corps 1941-1942

2 tank divisions (1 division was comprised of 11.343 men, 413 tanks)
1 motorized division
1 motor regiment
And supporting units
In total: 37.200 men and 1108 tanks
The tanks which were used varied from very light to very heavy. The most important types in the summer of 1941 were:

Russia's Field Army is Stationed Far to the West in the Field

General Andre Eremenko: 'Cavalry makes more of an impression than tanks'

Soviet tank weapon 1941

Type	Weight	Crew	Canon	Armory	Speed
T-26	10.3	3	45 mm	16 mm	18.6 mph
BT-7	13.8	3	45 mm	20 mm	33.2 mph
BT-7M	14.65	3	45 mm	20 mm	38.5 mph
T-28	28	6	76 mm	30 mm	22.9 mph
T-35	50	10	76mm 45 mm (2x)	30 mm	18.6 mph
T-34	30.9	4	76 mm	45mm	34.2 mph
KV-1	47.5	5	76 mm	75 mm	21.7 mph

(The KV-2, which suits the mobile artillery more is not included in these statistics).

Aside from the tanks, the Red Army had 13 cavalry divisions (9.249 men each) at its disposal, which were distributed over 4 cavalry corpses (19.000 men each, with 128 tanks). In addition, one could use five air corpses, comprised of 15 brigades (3.000 men per brigade), 76 artillery regiments, 15 heavy artillery battalions, and dozens of anti-tank units. Overall, the forces were comprised of 303 divisions, about 4.9 million troops.

The Clash of Titans

That a huge clash awaited both the Wehrmacht and the Red Army was evident; 170 divisions of the enormous Soviet army were stationed immediately at the border. It concerned 103 infantry divisions, 40 tank divisions (20 mechanized corpses! of 29 in total!), 20 motorized divisions (of 29!), 7 cavalry divisions, and a whole range of supporting units and special units, such as border garrisons. However, these numbers do not tell the whole story. Not all units were able to operate at full strength and there was also movements between troops. For instance, the Soviet infantry was at its full strength along the northern part of the eastern front (11.985 men per division at the Leningrad front), but not in other places, such as the Baltic states (8.712 men), the western front (Belarus 9.327 men), the Kiev region (8.792 men), and the southern front (Odessa 8.400 men). In addition, the individual weapons of the soldiers were not entirely in order. Between 80 and 90% of the men owned a personal gun, however, logistically speaking, matters were less fortunate. Many divisions only had 25 to 30% of the required vehicles at their disposal.

Even among the mechanized forces they were grasping at straws. Around 17.000 tanks in total were stationed in the border regions, but again, these numbers do not tell the entire story. No less than 15.000 of those were light tanks, 370 were middle class and heavy tanks, and only 1.475 tanks could be defined as new

Operation 'Barbarossa' commenced with a vulnerable railway plan

middle class/heavy tanks. In practice this meant that, of the 20 mechanized corpses, only 8 corpses had modern tanks at their disposal, of which the illustrious T-34 tank was most important. The T-34, which became available shortly before operation 'Barbarossa', had a great balance between speed, armoury, and fire power, and moved swiftly across the terrain. The Germans were fortunate in knowing that most Soviet tank crews barely had any experience with the T-34's, which resulted in the loss of many of these tanks due to human error. Most Soviet troops who previously served had used the T-26, a completely different tank, and could hardly take advantage of the experience with regards to the T-34. In addition, there were very few T-34's when the war started. The numbers vary from 1.000 to 1.400.

Although they were not at full strength, a formidable army was stationed at the border, and many other units were on their way, among which the 22nd army from the Ural district, the 16th from Central Asia, and the 19th from the northern parts of the Caucasus. The Soviets strategy was to immediately halt a possible attacker at the border, in order to control the attack with troops from the second echelon. Thus ensuring the war would then continue wherever the Soviets chose. From north to south the front had been divided into 4 sectors: the

Baltic front, where the 8th and 11th army were stationed at the front line, and the 27th in the depth. The western front, where the 3rd, 10th, and 4th armies were stationed at the first line, and where the 13th was used as a reserve; the central front west of Kiev, with the 5th, 6th, 26th, and the 12th armies; and the 21st, 16th, and 19th armies north and south of the capital of Ukraine, in order to meet the southern front (Odessa) with the 9th army. The 23rd army was stationed around Leningrad, and the 20th at Moscow. Not only the infantry divisions and the special border troops were stationed at the most western part of the front. A large number of the mechanized troops were also stationed there: the mobile units and the tank troops - 49 to 62 miles from the front line. The enormous depth of the Soviet Union, was, as a result, barely used due to the chosen offensive strategy. At the Pskov, Zhitomir, and Berdichev line, the second echelon of the mechanized corps was stationed. The western corps were ordered to 'halt' the rise of the German 'Blitzkrieg' and the second echelon was ordered to waltz over the marching troops in order to allow the Soviet Army (and communism) to move westward.

The Catastrophic Consequences of Moscow's Offensive Strategy

The Germans were also optimistic. On 23 June, when the war was one day old, field marshal Von Brauchitsch arrived in Angerburg, East Prussia, at the OKH headquarters - the supreme command of the army. He got straight to the point when general Paulus, the subsequent commander of the 6th army in Stalingrad, gave a presentation. 'Well Paulus, how long will this campaign last?' Von Brauchitsch asked. Paulus' answer was quick and determined: 'Russia will be destroyed in six to eight weeks'. The Germans were confident, and they had reason to be. The Red Army's setup offered great opportunities for the Germans. The 'Blitzkrieg' strategy, which had been tested in the west and had worked magnificently against the French, could be fully utilized here. By pushing through the Soviet Union's vastness, large units could be surrounded and cut off from the hinterland. Great quantities of men and weapons could be disabled here. Afterwards one would be able to move forward.

The consequences of the Soviets 'forward defence' strategy, and the success of the German 'Blitzkrieg', can be seen in the Soviets' losses and the Germans' expansion of territory, which followed as a result of the German attack. The Germans had difficulty keeping track of the statistical losses and continuously had to adjust the number. A number of 'Kessels' (encirclements/ surroundings)

German panzer troops march forward, Soviet infantry surrenders

took centre stage here; Bialystok-Minsk (a double encirclement), Smolensk, Uman, Gomel, Kiev, and Vyazma-Bryansk. Here, the bulk of the Soviet border army was defeated. The frequent use of the word 'systematic' in German daily progress reports, such as 'Die Wehrmachtsberichte', was remarkable. The papers were much like a broken record in that regrard. On 23 June, the attack was already reported to have progressed systematically and successfully. The next day the same message was repeated, and on the 25th it was stated that everything had progressed 'so favourably that major success could be expected'. On 26 June, victory in the battle for the border of Berlin was already claimed, which was a servere exaggeration. The battle would continue for weeks.

A series of 'Sondermeldungen' reported that Vilnius and Kaunas had been overrun, and on 28 June the first 'Kesselslag' was mentioned: Bialystok, where two Russian armies were stuck. In hindsight, the first German reports about the Soviet losses were child's play considering what would still come: 40.000 prisoners of war, 600 pieces of artillery, 2.233 tanks, and 4.107 planes, although the last two figures already indicated what was happening in the border area. Especially if one considers that at that time, the losses, for instance concerning the German air force, were up to 150 planes.

On 30 June the city of Lviv fell and two days later

the number of prisoners at Bialystok ran up to 100.000 men; more prisoners than had been reported for the entire front. The city of Riga was run over and shortly after the new 'overall' numbers appeared: 160.000 prisoners of war between 22 June and 1 July 1941, in addition to 2.330 pieces of artillery, 5.774 tanks, and 4.725 defeated planes. On 3 July the conclusion of the Bialystok encirclement campaign was announced, which would later be talked about as similar to the encirclement campaigns at the city of Minsk, on 5 July. This campaign was said to have had 20.000 Soviet 'defectors'. On 6 July, the number of prisoners of war at the capital of Belarus had risen up to 52.000, which eventually would end up to be (11 July, 1941) 323.898 prisoners of war, 3.332 tanks, 1.809 pieces of artillery, with which the total amount of Soviet losses in prisoners had gone over 400.000, in addition to 7.615 tanks, and more than 4.000 pieces of artillery. A few days before, the OKW reported that the Dnepr River had been reached, and on 13 July, 1941 the Stalin line, a series of reinforcements straight through the western part of the Soviet Union, was breached.

Millions of Red Army Soldiers Perish During the 'Kessel' Campaigns

The reports became more triumphant as days passed. On 17 July one stated that at Smolensk the final Soviet reserves had been used, and on 2 July, precisely one month after the start of the breach, the first German bombers flew above Moscow and bombarded the town. The 'Wehrmachtsberichte' reported on the 25th, using their familiar word 'systematic' again. The battle for Smolensk was in full swing, but more to the south, at Kiev, a new 'Kessel' took place. Bessarabia was officially declared as conquered on the 29th, and the breach of the Stalin line was again claimed on 6 August. Around that time the number of war prisoners had risen to nearly 900.000 men. When, on the 7th, the situation at Smolensk was assessed, this number quickly increased. More than 300.00 troops, 3.205 tanks, and many other material fell into German hands. The Kessel at Uman also

Die Wehrmacht

HERAUSGEGEBEN VOM OBERKOMMANDO DER WEHRMACHT

A train with Russian prisoners

made the news. Initially, the report said 30.000 prisoners of war. However, a day later, the number had risen to over 100.000 men. The fact that the ones killed in action were hardly mentioned in the reports was remarkable, but these numbers were also astronomical. At Uman, this number was estimated at 200.000 men, and at Gome, another 84.000 men fell into German hands. This led to a report on 22 August, when the campaign was two months old, that stated 1.250.000 prisoners of war, in addition to 14.000 tanks, 15.000 pieces of artillery, and 11.250 planes, of which 5.633 were destroyed on the ground. 'Systematic' was once again the word used by the OKW on 2 September. Barely two weeks later the number increased again during the 'Kessel' at Kiev, with 150.000 prisoners of war on 21 September, which increased to 665.000 men on 27 September, in addition to 8.84 tanks and 3.718 pieces of artillery. The long line of successes ended late 1941, when a hasty and sloppy established Soviet counter offensive in Vyazma- Bryansk resulted into another disaster similar to the 'Kiev-Kessel', only a lot less well-known. By 14 October, it was evident that at Semjon Konstantinovitsj Timosjenko's offensive, no less than 500.000 Soviet soldiers had lost their lives, and this number was adjusted to 657.948 prisoners of war, 1.241 tanks, and 5.369 pieces of artillery. On 10 November, the Germans counted 3.632.000 Soviet prisoners of war. Aside from the famous Kessel campaigns, there were also endless smaller fights, which were very bloody as well. Some of these never reached the public eye, such as the 30.000 Soviet losses at Velikiye Luki on 27 August, 1941, the 13.000 men at Dnepropetrovsk on 29 September, the 13.0000 men at the mouth of the Dnepr on 5 October, and the cumulative losses of the, to the Crimea retreating Soviet troops, who on 3 November, 1941 had lost 53.175 men to captivity, in addition to 230 tanks, and 218 pieces of artillery.

Main Kessel Campaigns 1941 in Soviet Prisoners of War

Kiev	665.000 men
Vyazma-Bryansk:	657.948 men
Bialystok/Minsk	323.898 men
Smolensk	310.000 men
Uman	103.000 men
Gomel	84.000 men

(The total amount of prisoners of war between 22 June, 1941 and 10 November, 1941: 3.632.000 men.

Prisoners experience a hellish journey, many will never return

Logistics were problematic during the Russian Campaign. Pictured is a bridge at Kiev across the Dnepr which was bombed by the Soviets

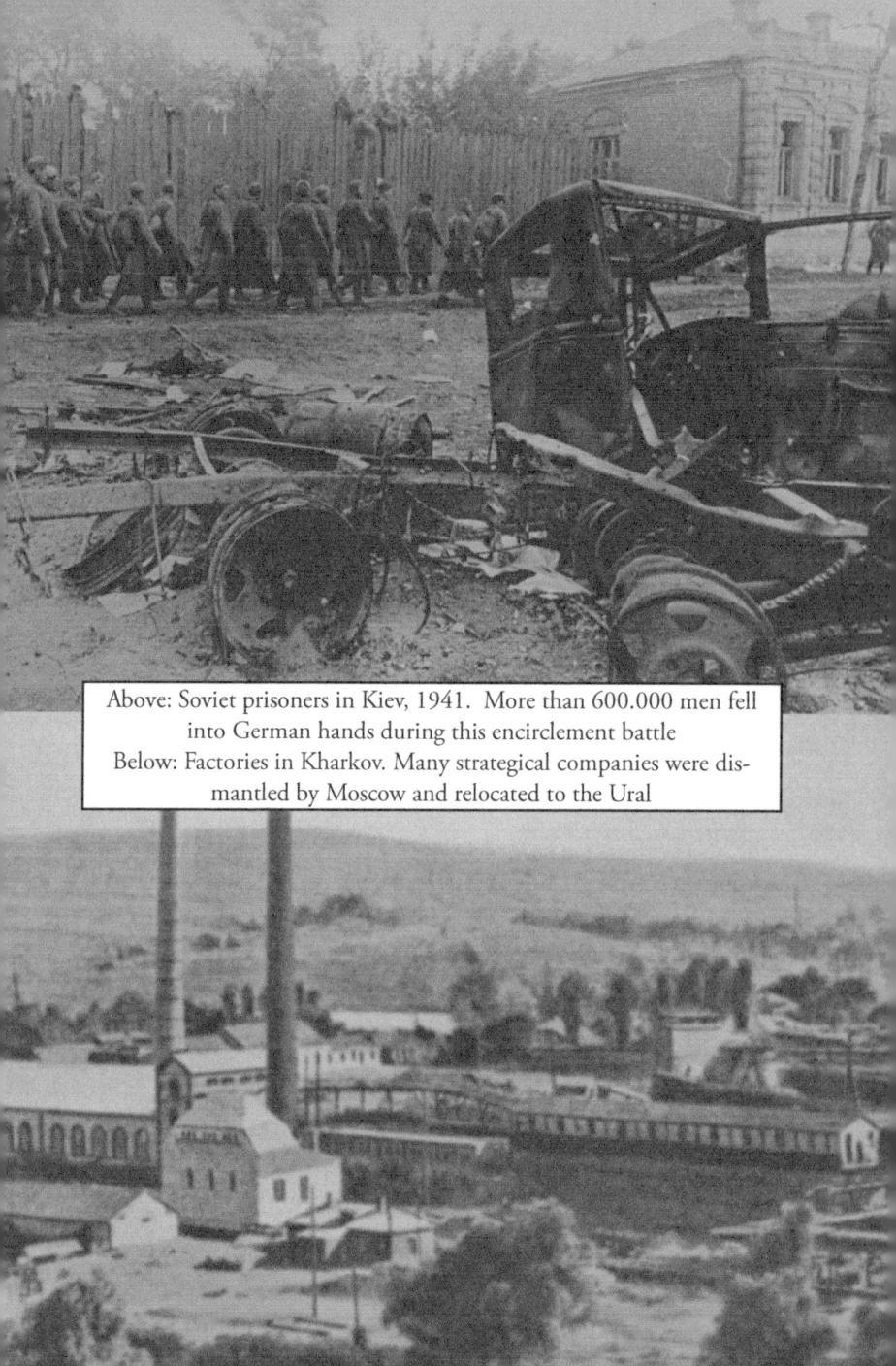

Above: Soviet prisoners in Kiev, 1941. More than 600.000 men fell into German hands during this encirclement battle
Below: Factories in Kharkov. Many strategical companies were dismantled by Moscow and relocated to the Ural

The material losses were also astronomical:

Material Losses Soviet Union between 22 June and 22 August, 1941

Tanks: 14.000
Artillery: 15.000
Airplanes: 11.250 (of which 5.633 on the ground)

From these figures we can also conclude that the Red Air force faced terrible losses. It was calculated that more than 17.000 planes were destroyed in 1941, mostly because the airports were located far to the west. Unfortunately, in the years to come the losses would remain astronomical (in 1942 the losses were the lowest, with 12.000 planes). However, the Soviet aircraft industry was still running. More than 600.000 workers in total would be deployed to maintain the aviation industry of the Soviet Union.

Economic Warfare: the Campaign for 'Lebensraum'

The destruction of Soviet forces was a prerequisite for Hitler's grand plan. In January 1941, Hitler already noted:

'The enormous Russian empire houses boundless resources. Germany needs to rule this on an economic and political scale [..] in order for Germany to have the means to fight against other continents in the future, enabling it to never be defeated by anyone again. After we have completed this mission, Europe will hold its breath.'

Hitler's ideology focused, with regard to foreign policy, on two pillars, as German historian Eberhard Jaeckel stated. One was the war against the Jews, which played a significant role during the crusade against Bolshevism, in light of the fact that Hitler considered it to be a 'Jewish matter'. The attack on the Soviet Union was, as a result, of great consequence to the Russian Jews, who were hunted down and murdered by the 'Einsatzgruppen' of the SS and the SD, that operated behind the front. Hundreds of thousands of Jews fell victim to them. In addition, there was a hunt for communists and political commissioners.

The other pillar of Hitler's policy was the desire for 'Lebensraum': a living space for the German people. Influenced by geopolitical thinkers of his time: Friedrich Ratzel, Rudolf Kjellen, Karl Haushofer, Oskar von Niedermayer and others, Hitler pursued a 'Grosswirtschaftsraum', allowing the country, which lacked raw materials, to become self-sufficient. This led to the idea of creating a Kernraum-Europe, where the geo-politicians dreamt of a cooperation between Germany (as country of knowledge), Russia (as supplier of men), in a pact with Japan (as fleet). However, Hitler never intended to share the loot. The 'Generalplan Ost', which had been thought through by the reichssicherheitshauptamt (Reich Security Main Office), in the cooperation with scientists such as Prof. Konrad Meyer-Hetling, Walter Christaller, and Heinrich Wiepking-Jürgensmann, paints a different picture. Hitler's plans for Eastern Europe did not speak of cooperation but of suppression, coupled with an exploitation strategy, and plans of genocide. The Generalplan Ost included a radical reform of the territory in Eastern Europe in favour of the German 'Grosswirtschaftsraum' and was in fact nothing other than a direct colonization of the region.

Scientist Walter Christaller concocted the 'Generalplan Ost'.

Professor Konrad Meyer-Hertling, scientific employee who worked on the SS' plans for Russia. Pictured on the right is a photo from his judicial file during the Neurenberg trials. Nevertheless, he was still successful after 1945

Konrad Meyer during his after-war trial

Above: German troops before Leningrad
Below: The Red Army moves west for the Wolchov offensive

Above: German troops at the fortress of Brest-Litovsk 1941
Below: Soviet soldiers from border defences have been captured and were literally fumigated

From Ostwall to Generalplan Ost

In order to provide some insight into the far-reaching plans, Dr. Wetzel, who was connected to the 'Reichsministerium für die besetzen Ostgebiete' that worked with the RSHA, had an interesting assignment. Dr. Wetzel worked out a plan to depopulate certain strategical areas, where the inhabitants were considered 'racially unwanted' ('rassisch Unerwünschten). At first it appeared that Hitler was satisfied with the so-called 'Ostwall', an area east of Germany where the slaves had been driven out. However, in October, 1929 this plan was replaced by a more ambitious and crueller one. Here it mostly concerned the Baltic region before and at Leningrad, and the Crimea. Those areas were supposed to be 'reconquered' for the Germans; German authorities spoke of the 'Festigung Deutsches Volkstums'. In the Baltic states and Leningrad (soon to be called 'Ingermanenland'), this plan was legitimized through an old-Teutonic presence in the region. In the

Above: 'The Holocaust of Bullets'
Below: The besieged Leningrad which the Germans wanted to call Ingermanenland

meantime, the Germans wanted to place the Tyrolean's on the Crimea (soon to be called 'Gotengau'), who would fit in there because landscape and climate was similar to their native terretory. In doing this, Hitler solved the dispute with Italy concerning Tyrol, and killed two birds with one stone.

The consequences of these plans were barely foreseen. To 'clear' the new land for the Germans, 31 million people had to be deported - later, different but also astronomical numbers were mentioned. For deportation the Germans had become interested in Western Siberia, where the unfortunate souls were shipped off to. The plans from the 'Generalplan Ost' did not only concern Russia, but also occupied Poland, which the Germans had renamed in the 'Generalgouvernement'. Here too, the Germans would go on a rampage. In total, about 80 to 85% of the Polish inhabitants were deported. For the western parts of the Ukraine and Belarus these numbers were 64 to 75%. The rest was allowed to stay, however, they would have to be 'germanisiert' (turned into German citizens). It is interesting to note that Dr. Wetzel was concerned about the quantaty of 'Slavic' people - who would move to western Siberia. To Germany this was 'unfortunate'. On the other hand, Dr. Wetzel understood that they could not simply 'eradicate' these inhabitants as they had done with the Jews.

Time was kind to the victims. In January, 1942 Konrad Meyer was put to work by Himmler, the head of the SS, to work out the Generalplan. In May, relatively quickly, the work was in writing. However, the enormous transformation of the region would have to be carried out step by step and take about 25 years. After statistical research done by the RSHA under the leadership of Dr. J. Beyer, the plans for deportation were as follows:

Polish territory invaded annexed by Germany	6 to 7 million people
Baltic nations	3 million people
Generalgouvernement	7 million people
Galicia/ Ukraine	6 to 7 million people
Belarus	4 to 5 million people

German Deportation Plans Eastern-Europe in Millions of People

Interestingly enough, Beyer stated that the Jews in the region, about 5 million people, would have to be evacuated. This report originates from February, 1943. From preserved reports drawn up by the Einsatzgruppen we know that those days a large part of the so-called 'Holo-

German propaganda, communism as 'Jewish implement'

caust of bullets (the destruction of the Jewish community in Russia) had already been carried out. The scientists who had been working for the SS denied or ignored these reports, or they simply did not know what was going on behind the Russian front. Here, the secrecy within the SS concerning the Jewish fate plays a role. The deportation of the Jews in Russia coexisted with the earlier plans for the Jews in Poland, where for some time one spoke of placing the Jews in a 'Reichs-Ghetto'. This ghetto would be stationed southwest of the City of Lublin and become an enormous 'Judenreservat'. Later on, this 'Reichs ghetto' at the border of Russia was considered a risk, which resulted in the abandonment of the plan.

Migration

On an economical scale this would have severe consequences. Nazi-Germany had set its eyes on large pieces of cultural landscape, which eventually could be used by German farmers and Industry. The 'Generalplan Ost' supplied 700.000 km2 of new settlements for the 'Deutschum' in Eastern Europe. If we look at the fact that Nazi-Germany (in 1938) had 538.000 km2 at its disposal, the impact of the plans becomes evident. Millions of Germans, about 45.000 to 50.000 per year, would migrate to the new areas. The plan was an important point on the agenda, until the turning point at the battle for Stalingrad, where Paulus' 6th army, and ten thousand additional troops from alliances perished. At that point it became evident that Himmler's ambitious plans would likely never see the light of day. It remained relatively small measures, such as the repatriation of the so-called Lithuanian-Germans, who returned home from the oc-

PLANUNG und AUFBAU im OSTEN

herausgegeben von: Der Reichskommissar

für die Festigung deutschen Volkstums

Stabshauptamt

German propaganda for the 'germanisering' of the east

DEUTSCHE LANDBUCHHANDLUNG·BERLIN SW 11

Above: after successful campaigns roaming through an enormous country
Below: Not all Germans believed in the 'Lebensraum' politics

cupied areas of Poland, in addition to the first German 'Siedlungsgebied' under the name of 'Hegewald, in the fall of 1942.

In the southern parts of the Ukraine, the area of 'Halbstadt' was added later. In Poland, which was occupied by the Germans, migrations also took place, especially around Lublin and Zamość. The Höhere SS und Polizeiführer (HSSPF) SS-Obergruppenführer F.W. Krüger characterized these movements as practice runs for the future. It was not easy because the Polish inhabitants feared the same fate as the Jews and resisted. The migration of the Crimea actually never took place. The stubborn defence of the Sevastopol fortress, the Soviet counter offensives, and landings from sea, created a turbulent situation which was unsuitable for migration.

A physical implementation of the Deutschtum therefore never took place, however, enormous areas in the Soviet Union were overrun. The Germans had an eye on the Ukraine and were determined to get their hands on it since it was, by far, the most important economic area.

Agricultural Posibilities in Western Ukraine

In a special brochure issued by the Oberkommenado der Wehrmacht in 1941 (heft 49) titled 'Die Ukraine und das Baltenland' the remarkable history of the Ukraine was commemorated. The Germans were fascinated with the history and fate of the Ukraine, to an extent. It was possible they felt a certain affinity. The Ukrainians were the largest people in Europe that did not own land. According to the Nazi's this was due to the fact that the Ukraine was a typical transit country, where Asian hordes constantly struck. For example, the Mongols (1240), and later the Tartars. Soviet-Russia, Stalin, and the communists were also held accountable for the subordinate role that Ukraine played in history. Furthermore, the Polish inhabitants played a role. According to the OKW, the farmers in Europe had nowhere else been as subju-

Above: Soviet civilians in the Ukraine, the breadbasket of the Soviet Union
Below: Ukraine 1941, the population is working on the roads under German supervision

gated as under the control of Poland. After the peace of Brest-Litovsk, and the collapse of the tsarist rule, a new opportunity for the Ukraine was born. However, in 1921 with the peace of Riga, the Ukraine was one again distributed, now among Poland and Russia.

In the 'völkische' world view of the Nazi's, where the farmer's life was praised, a certain kind of sympathy arose for the Ukrainians: with their simple lives, and clean villages (in comparison to the, according to the OKW, 'dirty' Russian villages) where poverty was cheerfully worn. The Ukrainians were very religious, mostly Greek-orthodox. However, their desire for freedom was dangerous to Nazi Germany. This pride extented to their lineage of slaves and Norsemen. After the fall of Poland in 1939, where the Red Army contributed from 17 September, the Eastern areas of Poland were added. It concerned the areas around Rovno, Volhynia, Brest and Pinsk; a vast but poor area. In comparison to the western part of Poland, it was hardly industrially developed, and the population, to European standards, knew a remarkably low quality of live. It was predominantly an agricultural area. In the areas that bordered the Ukraine, 93.000 km2, lived 8 million people, while another 101.800 km2 of Belarus receded, with approximately 5 million inhabitants. The Ukraine itself counted around 31 million inhabitants in 1939 and covered, before the annexation of Polish territory, 445.300 km2. Parts of especially western Ukraine existed of farmland, forest-steppe, where cities like Kamenev, Podolsk, Vinnytsia (where the Führer headquarters would be established), Zhitomir, Poltava, and Kirovograd were most famous. Aside from a sugar industry, there was little industrial activity. The Black Sea area was characterized by wine growing, and the harbours secured opportunities for supplies.

Industry in Eastern Ukraine

However, eastern Ukraine was industrially developed, with cities like Zaporozhye, Dnepropetrovsk, Stalino, Voroshilovgrad, and Kharkov, where one could find heavy industry and blast furnaces. In the Don-Volga area, with dominant cities Rostov and Stalingrad, industry could be found in the southern parts, and the cultivation of wheat in the north. A mingled landscape of industry and agriculture existed at the northern edge of the Ukraine with Russia around Voronezh, Tambov, Orel, Kursk, Sumy, and Tschernigow. This was an area with forest-steppe, where most of the forest was removed to make room for agriculture. A lot of heavy industry centered around the Donets Basin, and the city of Krivoy Rog (198.00 inhabitants) was the most populous area of the Soviet Union. Here, important strategical industries were stationed to aid the weapon industry, such as coal mining at Meshewsk, Pawlograd, and Nowomoskowsk (the Stalino area),

German occupation, Kharkov, 1941

in addition to lignite at Cristoforo and Weselo-Ternowsk, and manganese at Nikopol, all linked to a convenient location for distribution, among others via the Dnepr. Two thirds of the total Soviet iron industry was placed in the Donets base.

The industrialization resulted into strong urbanization. The Soviet Union urbanized quickly. In 1926, 18, 5% of the inhabitants lived in the cities, in 1939 this was 36, 2%. The most important cities in terms of agriculture and industry of the Soviet Union were:

Inhabitant Numbers of the Large Cities in the Ukraine

Kiev	846.000 inhabitants
Kharkov	833.000 inhabitants
Odessa	604.000 inhabitants
Dnepropetrovsk	501.000 inhabitants
Stalino	462.000 inhabitants

All these cities fell into German hands in 1941.

Even after the failed attack on Moscow, a number of territorial and military successes followed in 1942, Don and Donets, at Kalach, the conquest of Rostov, the march to the Caucasus, and the threatning of the Soviet oilfields. It was only in the fall and winter of 1942, during the battle for Stalingrad, that it became clear that the entire edifice of the Nazi's was much more instable than it seemed. The turning point had slowly set in. The Soviet Union stumbled, but recovered slowly. How was it possible for Stalin to recover from such terrible setbacks?

The answer can partly be found in the attackers themselves: the German army. The 'Wehrmacht' had never experienced a campaign that lasted longer than six weeks. Operation 'Barbarossa' would be something else completely: a war of initiation, with its own problems. Let us focus on the most important facets; first the logistics, crucial to every war. Both the railways and the motorways had their own problems.

Defeated Soviet tanks at Voronezh

The Soviet Union: a Logistical Nightmare

The road network of the Soviet Union was in terrible condition. Normally speaking panzer units could march for four days without supplies. On the power-hungry Soviet road network this could only be done for two days. The supply and dispatch was usually carried out with trucks. This brought forward an enormous logistical problem. Germany had been able to use of the railway system against France. This was different in Russia because its width tracks diverged (89 mm wider) from their own. During the Poland campaign, the German high command insisted on taking hold of the strategic (railway) bridges, such as at Grudziadz, or the Weichsel Bridge at Tczew, and the railway tunnel underneath the Jablanica Mountain. The railway tracks in Poland were mostly used to transport supplies to the front, in order to transport them via the, according to the Germans, 'grosstransportraum' to the east. After the fall of Poland, the Polish railway system had been integrated into the German system, which was essential for shipping supplies to the eastern front. Any experience the Germans had with the Russian railway system stemmed from large scale transports of raw materials to Nazi-Germany through Moscow, and semi-finished products and goods from Germany to Russia. Transportation via railways travelled from transfer points where one could switch between the width of tracks, which happened frequently at Brest, and at Żurawica at Przemyśl. Petroleum was transported via Romania.

In terms of railways the Germans had taken a big risk from day one. The railway network in the Generalgouvernement, occupied Poland, was less sophisticated than in Germany, and fell short in many instances. The Germans tried to overcome these problems with regards to operation 'Barbarossa', with the so-called 'Aufbau Ost': an order on August 9, 1940, which stated that the 'Reichsban' and the 'Generaldirektion der Ostban' needed to improve the capacities in the area. On 10 May, 1941, shortly before the Russian campaign, these improvements had to be finished. The result was tremendous pressure. It is interesting to note that with the additional plan of attack, the discussion of the railway tracks was sidelined. Consequently, preparations did not go beyond

The border crossing from Baltic territory to Russia

the Generalgouvernement. In cooperation with 'Organisation Todt', German pioneer units and Polish companies worked ferociously. When operation 'Barbarossa' commenced, six railway tracks were ready for the attack on the east and were frequently used. During the preparations made for 'Barbarossa' the use of the railway tracks was already discussed: 17.000 trains, with a maximum use of 48 trains a day.

The German idea that they would take hold of enough railway material in order to keep travelling on the wider tracks in Russia was dangerous. Additional locomotives and trains were not provided. This occurred in spite of warnings from German experts, such as General Von Lossberg. Hitler never took the concerns seriously. A month after the start of the Russian campaign, the German general staff already cried out to the railway pioneers to get the logistics going. Other technical matters also played an inhibitory role. For instance, the Russian locomotives ran on different coals, and in Russia, a specialized network for railway employees existed who were to keep the tracks free from snow. This infrastructure collapsed when Germany invaded Russia.

The Three Regiments of the 'Grosstransportraum'

As a result, a huge burden fell on the shoulders of the transport units of the German army. As we saw before, these were organized in the so-called Grosstransportraum and were comprised of three regiments with the numbers 602, 605, and 616, which were also divided into smaller units. These units had first seen the light of day in Poland, and had suffered relatively heavy losses. The units were, after battle in France, and with an eye on operation 'Barbarossa', heavily reinforced. From 20.000 tons, tonnage increased to 60.000 tons, with thousands of trucks in each regiment. This threefold increase was in fact a too optimistic assessment of the problems which would occur, because the transport convoys were vulnerable to attacks. In addition, the fleet was composed of hundreds of trucks, which were taken from the opponents, or simply confiscated from the bourgeoisie. In

France alone, the Germans had already seized 13.000 trucks. The maintenance was also a significant problem. Although there were, in addition to the three regiments, a range of other transport departments, such as the NSKK, from the posts and other organizations (fuel had its own transport), logistics were vulnerable. There were too few trucks. The OKW calculated that on a yearly basis, 150.000 trucks had to be produced to maintain the transport. However, they were only able to produce 39.000 trucks. Several places at the front suffered an

The population of the Ukraine had not forgotten about the 'holodomor', and was, as a result, not necessarily against the 'Wehrmacht'

acute shortage of fuel and ammunition in 1941, such as at the Pz.gruppe 1 at the southern part of the eastern front. On 13 October there was a serious shortage, on 17 October the OKW spoke of a 'catastrophic situation', and on the 20th the entire march came to a halt due to a lack of ammunition and fuel. The commanding general, Von Rundstedt, and the OKW did everything in their power to start things up again. Food and medicine were taken off trucks to make room for ammunition and fuel. They also considered making use of the Bow River in terms of logistics, and tried to make use of the Black sea via the harbour of Nikolayev.

Logistical problems were also present during the exploitation of the occupied territory. The German planners had conveniently assumed that, especially the Ukrainian agricultural land (including the trucks, tractors, and mowers) would fall into German hands unharmed. Considering the fact that the Red Army tried to destroy everything during their retreat, this was a far too optimistic assessment. There were half a million tractors active in the Soviet Union alone, and for the acquisition of the harvest, at least 20.000 trucks were needed.

The Russian territory was substanial and the catastrophic state of the roads during the mud season were harmful to the results. Until then the Germans were accustomed to transporting damaged vehicles and tanks back to Germany for repairs. This had been an option due to the short campaigns, but now this was a lot more complicated. In fact, it was, considering the existing capacity, only possible to march to Minsk. Before Smolensk, logistics had already been problematic. The result was that the march forward took a lot longer than intended.

Logistics had been divided at the 'Grosstransportraum', which was comprised of the regiments 602, 605, and 616

Above: Dozens of provisional signs display the routes for several units in Smolensk. In the background a soviet building is transformed into the 'Ostlandhotel'

Below: German troops deliver fuel for the 'Blitzkrieg', Smolensk, 1941

A War for Oil Waged 'Without Fuel'

From the start, the German fuel situation was concerning. After the First World War, the British politician Curzon believed that the Entente had won the war 'on a wave of oil'. The First World War had demonstrated that the armament and industrial production was just as important, if not more important than heroism in the field. Germany had, especially with regards to fuel, suffered from the blockage the Entente had placed on sea. In addition, Germany lacked, in terms of petroleum, raw materials. The paradox of Nazi Germany was that the fight for Lebensraum, which was also driven by a need for raw materials, could not be carried out due to a lack of oil. After the invasion of Poland, Germany focused on the Galicisch oilfields at Boryslav and Drohobych, in addition to smaller Austrian fields after the 'Anschluss', and significant oil reserves after the west campaign, with the occupation of Rotterdam, Antwerp, and La Rochelle.

The German 38-T tank with extra fuel, owned by the 7th panzer division

Future goals focused on Iraq and the Caucasus, two military goals which were ultimately not achieved after the German army got stuck about 12 miles before Groznyy and the oilfields of Chechnya. In Romania, things were different. Romania had become a more trustworthy ally to Nazi-Germany under the command of General Antonescu, and as a result the oilfields at Ploesti could be utilized for the German war economy. The oilfields belonged to the most heavily defended piece of airspace of Nazi-Germany. When the Soviets carried out an oil related air strike around Ploesti in August, 1941, Hitler personally ordered the destruction of the Soviet airbase in the Black Sea, and stressed for the acceleration of the march to the Crimea. Additionally, one tried to get the synthetic oil-industry going. Especially Hermann Göring, with his Vierjahrenplannen (four year plans), succeeded in creating a guiding line in the German oil production. Hitler's had suggestion of making Germany self-sufficient in 18 months, completely failed.

The Reichsführer-SS Himmler also experimented to his heart's content, and even tried to squeeze oil from pine needles. With a combination of experts, lead by I.G. Farben's front man Carl Krauch, a policy was finally established. However, oil would remain a major concern. Many commanders of tank troops admitted after the war that they had only been able to keep moving because of their secret supplies. With regards to fuel the ratio in comparison to the allied forces was 1:100.

Carl Krauch; a photo from his judicial file after the war.
His name is misspelled with a K.

The German War Industry was not suited for Mass Production

Although the 'Blitzkrieg' went hand in hand with modern day technology and strategy, the German economy was not modern at all. Industrial mass production hardly existed in Germany, which was mostly due to the fact that a large part of the German fleet was multifunctional, thus not suitable for mass production, in the way that, for instance, the United States was. In addition, as famous historians of the Bundesarchiv calculated, more than half of the German fleet was older than 10 years when the war commenced. Remarkably, the most modern lathes of the German industry were 4.000 American lathes, which they confiscated in Poland, in 1939. The shortages (sometimes even in coals, which Germany had plenty of), they tried to compensate for with the robbery spoils from occupied territories. Due to the strong expansion of the Wehrmacht before the Russian campaign, and the major losses suffered in 1941, the army's pressure on the working part of the men increased. The industry suffered from it, and they triend to compensate via the Arbeistzeinsatz. Even the food supply was under a lot of pressure. Something which also had to be fixed with the spoils of the war in the east. The Germans assumed that this would result in millions of deaths.

Problems among the Armed Forces: the Missing Feldhaubitze 18

The panzer weapon has gotten the most attention in history, which is partly justified. However, we must not forget that the bulk of the war was fought by a walking army, the 'landser' (German infantryman). And these soldiers often had to work without the support of tanks (which 'cut' through the enemy, after which the infantry had to purify the terrain – bloody handwork!) and heavily supported on the artillery. Consequently, it was a major setback that the standard howitzer, which should be at the disposal of the infantry divisions, the SFH 18 (schwere feldhaubitze 18), produced by Rheinmetal in Düsseldorf, and at Krupp in Essen, was not available to each unit. 1.469 were needed for operation 'Barbarossa' but they were 840 short. At the last minute one tried to fix this shortage, by increasing the production capacity via the MAN factories in Berlin, and the Skoda factories in Dubnica, Slovakia. However, this shortage could not quickly be fixed, and the German general staff was forced to make use of plundered canons from earlier campaigns. The French 'Feldkanone M97' was in fact most suited, however, most of the 860 canons had already been claimed by the majority of the competing corpses. As a result, 80 went to the Romanians, 410 to the Kriegsmarine, and Göring managed to get his hands on 371. Here, the ambitions of the chief of the Luftwaffe, who would eventually also receive a land army (Luftwaffe-infantry divisions), played a role, . As a result, the German army started the campaign against Russia with an understaffed artillery. What about the tanks?

Feldhaubitze 18

Hitler Believed the PzKw III Tank to be a 'Failure'

Up until that point the 'Blitzkrieg' had been carried by the German tank weapons and the motorized infantry. In Russia, the tank units and the panzer grenadiers were divided into four panzer groups (Pz. Gruppen), of which Pz. Gruppe 1 (General Hoepper) served at the Heeresgruppe (army group) Nord, the Heeresgruppe Mitte had the Pz. Gruppe 3 (General Hoth) and Pz. Gruppe 2 (General Guderian) at its disposal, while Pz. Gruppe 1 (Von Kleist) served at the Heeresgruppe Süd. The panzer troops expanded after the Poland and France campaigns. This was due to the successful operations in the campaigns mentioned above. In Poland, the German army had 2.800 tanks at its disposal, which were mostly of a light type. Nevertheless,they overran the Polish and successfully ended the campaign. The campaign against France, where more semi-heavy tanks were used, was a resounding success. British military historian Kenneth Maksey called it the 'most celebrated campaign in the world'. While the French had more, and in many respects, even better tanks than the Germans, the 'Blitzkrieg' tactics worked miraculously.

The German mobile warfare had its momentum, and that is how they ended up against the Soviet Union. However, a number of things were overlooked. Although they appeared to be stronger than ever, and the number of tank divisions had been doubled in 1941 in comparison to other previous years, they forgot that the number of tanks per division had been reduced considerably and that the 'Blitzkrieg' had, up to that moment, only been tested in short campaigns.

A number of things can also be said about the tank units themselves. It was already noted that the number of tanks per division had decreased, but what was worse was the fact that of the best tanks only a handful were present. At first it was the intention to have 2.160 PzKw tanks in the field on 18 July, 1941. In reality, the Germans had only produced 480 in 1941, and a mere 500 were available when operation 'Barbarossa' commenced. These tanks were also equipped with a 2 inch canon (pak 38) instead of the 3 inch (short barrel) that was supposed to be used. As commander of the 17th Pz.Div., F.M. von Senger und Etterlin, looking back, concluded that the 2 inch barrel was inadequate for the east front. The Soviets were often better equipped.

The bulk of the campaign was carried out with lighter tanks, such as the PzKw III of the MIAG firm, and Daimler Benz. However, this tank (Daimler Benz) had to be constantly upgraded (in existence were the PzKw III B, C, D, E, F, G, H, J, K, L, M, N, and a few special types) to withstand the test of time. Hitler himself believed the III to be an 'unsuccessful type'. About the PzKw I and II, which carried the 'Blitkrieg' in 1939 and 1949, we say nothing of substance. These were no match for the Soviets. The lines were supplemented with semi-heavy stolen Czech tanks that functioned relatively well during the early years of the east campaign, and comprised about a quarter of the tanks (Panzerkampfwagen 35 (t) and Panzerkampfwagen 38 (t), and also served for the Romanian and Hungarian army. The Germans also partly leaned on the Sturmgeschütz, the mobile artillery of Daimler-Benz and Krupp, which experienced an interesting development during the war. At first, there were relatively few available (548 pieces were produced in 1941), and the monthly production was relatively low.

Despite the victories the German losses were also enormous. The tank units also suffered. The losses in 1941 were as such:

German tanks between June 1941, and January 1942

June 1941	3.648 tanks
July 1941	3.530 tanks
August 1941	2.889 tanks
September 1941	2.262 tanks
October 1941	2.044 tanks
November 1941	2.480 tanks
December 1941	2.177 tanks
January 1914	1.803 tanks

In total the Germans lost 3.254 tanks and Sturmgeschützen in the period from 22 June, 1941 to 1 January, 1942. During the same time the army received 1.153 tanks and Sturmgeschützen as reinforcement. However, this meant that only a little more than 35% of the lost material had been replaced. The infantry also lost its force. In 1941 the army at the eastern front lost 1 million men, of which 600.000 were replaced. Here, the fight had also become a war of exhaustion.

Hitler Believed the PzKw III Tank to be a 'Failure'

The army moved continuously from logistical problems and fights with huge losses, to strategic goals that had to be reached. For the 'Heeresgruppe Mitte', for instance, traffic chaos was a large problem. Von Bock's unit was not disciplined enough to march forward, and at the River Bow, traffic chaos and congestion developed as a result. Sixteen quick divisions and 31 infantry divisions tried to move to the east. The tank troops of Heinz Guderian came to a standstill because the 'Grosstransportraum' could not reach across the River Bow. Here, similar to

Hitler believed the PzKw III tank to be a failure

at Von Rundstedt, the Germans called for emergency measures, and thus tanks were supplied from the air. The conquest of the major oil reserve at Baranovichi was fortunate for the 'Heeresgruppe Mitte'. Nevertheless, Guderian only had a supply of gas for 24 miles and ammunition for five days when he continued his march from the Dnepr to the east towards Smolensk. Supplies and deadlines became a dangerous game of cat and mouse.

A PzKw IV tank of the German army

Gerd von Rundstedt

The Red Army Stumbles

Destroyed Soviet planes

A Large Junk yard

The numbers did not lie. Every 31 miles the Germans marched forward, 20 to 30% of the tanks collapsed. This was partly due to new hostile action, but also because of exhaustion. The tanks had to be restored on site in Russia, which was not something that had been done before, and was thus not without problems. The number of failures also increased; for instance, at the 6th regiment, pz.div. 41 Czech T-35 tanks collapsed in September 1941 alone. The OKH, the supreme command of the army, immediately brought two new reserve divisions to the front: the 2nd and the 5th pz.D. The 'Korprückwärts' where 'Sicherungsdivisionen' were used to keep matters stable, had to deal with partisan activities and were urgently provided with French 'Beutepanzers'. An internal German report of the OKW from 23 July, 1941 spoke of a decrease in force of 50% within the tank divisions. This was also the case with the motorized divisions. The infantry would lose 80% of its force.

The word 'Winter' was taboo to Hitler. However, when on 11 October the first antifreeze reached the German troops, it became evident that this war could not be won. This led to new problems. By not acknowledging this fact on time, the German troops were not prepared for winter. Within the German strategy, 56 divisions were used for the occupation of the country (see annex 1). Two thirds of the German army was thus to return to Germany during the winter of 1941-1942. This all turned out differently. Before The Red Army kept its position in front of Moscow, and winter material would have to be urgently moved to the front. At the central front, the logistics ran through Gomel, where the transportraum had established a large storage facility. Up until 16 October, 1941, the kraftwagen transport regiment 616 had delivered 291.000 tons of goods, which was the equivalent of 680 trains. A huge accomplishment, but it was not enough. Via planes, the necessary winter supplies travelled east to the troops: 47.000 pairs of gloves, and 68.000 hats. The army troops now understood that because the word winter was avoided, a shortage of supplies would occur and, as a result, they decided to gather warm clothing themselves. For instance, one of the army

Graves of soldiers from the 9th panzer division, behind the graves the destroyed a PzKw III

groups had 30.000 snow shirts made and handed out to the troops. However, this was still not enough. In November, the German panzer generals stated that another 35% of the tanks could be deployed. Things were far worse for the non-armoured troops. Here only 15% of the vehicles could be used. The east front had turned into a large junk yard. The assumption is that in the winter of 1941-1942 about 100.000 cars and trucks died because of technical damage and a lack of spare parts.

The wear and tear of the material was enormous

Changing Direction, the German High Command Hesitates

The lack of homogeneity with regards to carrying out commands on German sides also played a role. In a certain sense the German army was constrained by its own successes. For instance, the city of Daugavpils, with its strategical bridges, quickly fell into the hands of the Heeresgruppe Nord. In addition, the encirclement battle at Bialystok soon ended successfully. These two successes also came with new questions. In the war diary of 'Oberkommando der Wehrmacht', the OKW, these successes are described as the so-called 'Sonderakte' (no. 66 and 67) dated 26 and 27 June (on the fourth and fifth day of the raid the course was already questioned!) where Hitler and his generals asked themselves if the successes at Bialystok were a sign that the armed forces should move to the south. After the conquest of Daugavpils, north from the front, it was questioned whether to march towards Leningrad or turn south. In Sonderakte 62 of the OKW's diary (KTB), Hitler stated that he believed the destruction of the hostile forces was more important than territorial goals. It showed Hitler had learned from Napoleon's lessons: that Moscow was not a target on its own, the same as Stalingrad had not been at the summer planning (Fall Blau) of 1942. On 3 July (Sonderakte 66), new doubts arose. The OKW determined that the decisions had to be made after the battle of Smolensk, and the main options were:

- March to the north east: Leningrad
- March to the east: Moscow
- March to the south east   Sea of Azov

'This will be one of the most difficult decisions to make during the campaign', Hitler noted in Sonderakte 66, and with it he hit the nail on its head. Simple sentences on paper equalled enormous changes and distances. For instance, the change of course from Smolensk to Kharkov meant a distance of 462 miles, and towards the south, to the Sea of Azov about 714 miles. Even in the 'Sonderakte', it was questioned if this could be done. An interesting assessment, and along the same lines as the Germans boosting their morale through Hitler stating that 'it was good that all the tanks and airplanes were destroyed at the start of the campaign because these could not have been replaced'. Hitler concluded that the Soviet Union had 'practically already lost the war'. ('Sonderakte' 67 of 4 July, 1941).

German cavalry, Russia 1941

Waffen-SS soldiers of the 'Totenkopf' division, Smolensk 1941

Overconfident until the End; the Small-Scale Attack on Moscow by the 4th army and the Pz.gruppe 4

'Sonderakte' 67 turned out to be a miscalculation. The Red Army was of a reasonable size. As a result, the army that survived the battles at the borders were enough to keep going. In addition, the Soviets quickly established new units. The encirclement battle at Kiev had delayed the march at the central front, however, on 5 September, a decision was finally made. All eyes were now on the Heeresgruppe Mitte for the attack on Moscow. Ten days later, the most important units of the Heeresgruppe Nord were on their way to meet the Heeresgruppe Mitte. The Germans determined that the actual siege of Leningrad would destroy the Soviet position in the north. The plan was not conquer the city, but to slowly strangle it in a starvation blockage. After the large-scale Soviet bombing campaign, a certain fear had erupted to enter the cities among the Germans (many deaths in Kiev by mines on 24 September). The Panzergruppe 4 was forced to hand

The Panzergruppe 4 was forced to give away half of its fast troops to the Heeresgruppe Mitte

over half of its fast troops to the Heeresgruppe Mitte. This had several tricky side effects. The encirclement ring around Leningrad was very wide, and the Soviets also remained in position at Orianienbaum on the coast, which resulted into the establishment of a long front line which had to be covered by the heeresgruppe Mitte. From the front around Ladoga and Wolchov, the Soviets continuously tried to break through the encirclement ring, so a strategic mobile reserve remained necessary, and 2 Pz. Div and 3 Gem. Divisions were left behind. These units were missed during the decisive battle for Moscow. In addition, the measures taken in Leningrad put the brakes on opening the 'north front' to Moscow. The Heeresgruppe Süd was not able to sufficiently help either. Here, Hitler forced the troops to turn south, towards Rostov and the basin of Donets and the Crimea. Political and economic goals were essentia, but it also meant that the Heeresgruppe Mitte was on its own.

Operation 'Taifun' Fails

The 'Kessel' battle at Kiev ended relatively late, at the end of September 1941. This meant that the attack on Moscow, operation 'Taifun', could begin on 2 October. The Heeresgruppe Mitte now had 3 armies and 3 panzer groups at its disposal. The start was very promising because shortly after the Kessel battle at Kiev, the success at Vyazma-Bryansk followe with astronomical Soviet losses (according to some historians the Soviet losses were bigger here than at Kiev). Even Stalin began to hesitate. In October all decisions were made. Stalin considered peace negotiations with the Germans via Bulgaria, and had even built new headquarters at the Volga, thinking about leaving Moscow. A massive relocation of the Soviet industry and ministries had already begun to take place. Risks were also taken in the east, where, primarily based on the information of spy Richard Sorge, it was decided to move the Asian units of the Soviet Union to the front at Moscow. The Germans were so convinced of their upcoming victory that it diluted the attack. Parts of the 9th army and pz.gruppe 3 circled back to the north and the direct attack on Moscow was left to a relatively limited force, the 4th army and the Pz.gruppe 4. On maps, the Soviets were forced to defend 186 miles of front from Kalinin to Kaluga with modest resources: 12 infantry divisions, and 16 pz. Brigades. Normally this would mean a relatively thinly occupied front. However, Soviet general Zjoekov, who previously had taken care of business at Leningrad, realized that the German motorized units which were the vanguard, depended on the few paved roads. The early start of a thaw period contributed to the delay of the march, and the loss of vehicles. The German army's overstretch became increasingly clear. While chief of press Otto Dietrich had already claimed the victory after Vyazma-Bryansk, the realistic Josef Goebbels put things on hold. He had already, in the back of his mind, taken into account that the war would not be decided in 1941 and warned for a disillusion if the expectations were too high.

Von Bock, the ambitious army group leader of the Heeresgruppe Mitte asked everything of his men and units. On 11 November, however, it was Von Bock himself who hesitates. The Heeresgruppe Mitte itself stated that reaching the Moscow canal was probably the best they could do. On 23 November, the reserves last infantry division was deployed. Some regiments counted but 250 soldiers. On 1 December,

Operation 'Taifun' Fails

Russian spy Richard Sorge

Fedor von Bock hesitated on 11 November, 1941 before Moscow

Von Bock asked the OKW the following question: attack or defend, and on 3 December, after the answer had never come, they reached the city, keeping a distance of 11 miles. Two days later, Zjoekov started the counter attack and the high-water mark of the battle was over. Halder warned for a new Marne-drama, but in temporary winter barriers, the Soviet attack on the western positions was waited out for summer. Interestingly enough, Hitler never took responsibility, insted changing course again on 22 November. He then felt that the priority was at the southern front and at Leningrad.

'Barbarossa', Beria, Purging and Terror

The Soviets had just enough breath to withstand the attack. The enormous preparations Moscow had taken before the war already paid off, even though, because of their own misfortune and shifted armies, they still almost lost. The Soviet defence budgets had, in the years before the war, been increased from 25,6% of the state budget in 1939 to 32,6% in 1949, to 43,4% in 1941. In addition, the war waged relentlessly, against the population, but also against the military. Famous and notorious were the Stalin purges of the army, just before operation 'Barbarossa'. Many experienced officers had been lost as a result. However, an advantage was the fact that a relatively young corps of officers was ready. Others believed that if the old guard (of the 48.773 commanders only 12.000 survived the purge), had been alive, the Germans had never been so successful. Again Stalin pun-

NKVD unit, which, with terror, maintained the political stability at the front and in the hinterland

Lavrentiy Beria stated that the Secret Service took drastic measures.

Dimitri Pavlov, executed on command of General Zjoekov

ished others for his failures and many officers lost their lives. Marius Broekmeyr, a Russian expert, made notes of their hearings. On 23 June, (one day after the raid!) general Kirill Meretskov and several others were arrested. He had to admit to being the leader of a group of 'military conspirators'. He was severely abused: 'Rodos broke his ribs'. The unfortunate rolled over the floor and tried to cure his unbearable pains with screams'. Secret service leader Lavrenty Beria admitted during his trial in 1953 that things had taken drastic turns. Prisoners were 'peed in the face'. General Stern was, in addition to other high generals, shot with his wife. Others disappeared in the Loebjanko prison and never returned. Generals were often replaced, such as General Pavlov by Timonsjenko. Zjoevov himself signed the execution order for Pavlov. His wife and five-year old son were banished to Siberia. According to historian Dirk W. Oetting, about 13.500 Russian soldiers were executed by the NKVD at the Battle for Stalingrad alone, in order to maintain discipline. The people who were not executed ended up in a punishment battalion. In total about 430.000 men would have served in such a unit, which gives an idea of the terror at and behind the front. However, we should not be surprised. Even before 1941, the communist regime had been responsible for at least twelve million deaths through murder and repression, especially in

General A.A. Vlassov chose the German side

the Ukraine. In the meantime, a scorching earth tactic was used. On 17 November, an official command had been given and 24 to 37 miles from the front everything had to be burned to the ground. Everything that was of strategic significance, such as the industry, was relocated. This was a logistical masterpiece. Overall, about 1,6 million railway wagons were relocated. Entire factories, including staff and families were relocated, and in 1942 the industry was up and running again. In total, about 18 million people were evacuated with the industry, in addition to 2.593 companies. Even cattle was relocated, on the spot 'cattle brigades' were formed that drove the animals east. Nothing was allowed to stay. The kolkhoz-system worked in the advantage of the Soviet authorities. Often the emphasis is placed on the Soviets who, with their (Siberian) counter attacks, had driven the Germans away at Moscow. In reality the Germans had already lost their advantage and their retreat was a fact when Zjoekov, and the known counter attacks of General A.A. Valssov, who would later on cross over to the Germans, took place.

The Third Reich: Skilled with Conquests, Bad with Consolidation

The preservation of the Soviet Union came, in addition to the enormous blood sacrifice made by the Red Army, from a mix of logistical, geographic, and military reasons, where a general underestimation of the power and size of the Soviet Union played a leading role. The Soviet characteristic to give it their all, and if they did not, the Soviet military safety services (NKVD), stood behind the front with field police battalions and killed everyone who retreated without orders, which played a significant role. In addition, the relocation of the industry, the launch of the American British material deliveries, in addition to the 'rücksightloze' mobilization of the home country, played a decisive role. The Germans did, for instance at the Donets coal basin, conquer important industrial and mining areas. However, the industry had been relocated or destroyed, the labour forces evacuated, and the mines had been flooded. It was a large shock when German experts visited the high quality iron ore and manganese mines of Krivoy Rog. The destruction they met mid-August 1941 restated each imagination. Equipment, even weighing more than 100 tons, had been evacuated, and of the 2000 electric motors of the blast furnaces of Krivoy Rog, only 50 remained. Fifty mineshafts had been blown up or flooded. The 'Bergbau' battalion mot. 26 was brought forward to reinstate things. The energy had to be supplied by plants that first had to be rebuilt again. The coals had to be mined at Stalino. The only industry that had been conquered when it was still more or less intact, were the steelworks at Mariupol. Although the Germans forced 24.000 workers from

The population of the heavily damaged Minsk tries to save themselves. People are hungry in the, by Germany occupied areas, but the word hunger was not allowed to be used

Ukrainian children welcome Nazi-Germany

Nazi ideologist Alfred Rosenberg

Above: German infantry at Stalino
Below: A Sturmgeschütz conquered by the Soviets

the kolkhoz to work in the factories, a mere 5 to 10% of the pre-war capacity would be reached.

When in 1943 the power could be generated from the (water plant) of Zaporozhye, and production was on track, the Red Army reconquered the industrial areas. The Third Reich was good with conquests but not so well with consolidation. Throughout the entire Third Reich several instances worked against and alongside each other. The industry was handled by the 'Reichsministerium für die besetzen Ostgebiet', of Nazi-ideologist Alfred Rosenberg, in addition to the 'Wirtschaftsstab Ost' of the army, Himmler's SS, and Hermann Göring's four year plans. Due to logistical problems, the occupation of the area had also not been successful. Although a considerable part of the Ukrainian population and those in the Baltic states considered the Germans to be liberators, the relations soon became tense again because the Germans made little room for the independence wishes of the population. The terror of 'Einsatzgruppen' and the 'Kommandostab Reichsführer-SS', and the administrative chaos in the hinterland, with famines and shortages, drove the population in the hands of the partisans. In turn, these partisans, fed by Moscow, carried forward a terror-like campaign, both against the German occupation and their own people.

The Stubborn, Tough Russian Soldier

How much people had misjudged the vitality of the Russians was also noted in the first SD report of the occupied areas of 2 January, 1942. This internal document (65 copies), addressed to Berlin (Geheime Reichssache!) read:

'After Lake Ladoga was frozen over, several persistent attacks on the ice to the south followed. Remarkable was the action of a unit on skis, who were very well trained and comprised of specially selected soldiers. This regiment had been armed with machine guns. Every man had brought four days' worth of equipment, among which chocolate and tobacco. The attack was disrupted by combined troops. It is typical that only a few days later two ski-battalions started another attack at the same place. The Soviet artillery was also very active around Leningrad and reached an unexpected size within some front sectors. This shows that the war industry of Leningrad is still function-

The Red Army Stumbles

al. The Russian air force also seems to have recovered from the first blows. At night, several airfields and road junctions were attacked. [..] the German command is constantly surprised by the toughness and persistence of the Russians, and their skills in establishing new formations and troop units. Devastated units and scattered soldiers quickly return to units and used 'rucksightlos'. The Russian ability to improvise is considered by Germans as decisive to preserve the Russian desire for resistance. [..] the Russian soldiers and workers of Leningrad distinguish themselves by 'tough perseverance".

Soldiers of the Red Army carrying a mortar

Above: the Red Army recovers from the first blows
Below: Soviet panzer troops march west

Above: Wehrmacht 1941, increasing losses and a never occurring collapse of the Soviet Union
Below: On a logistical scale the war had definitively stranded

Epilogue

Operation Barbarossa is the history of hubris. Stretched by earlier successes, badly informed by their own intelligence services, and with an army filled with defects and deficits, and a weak logistical system and economy, Nazi Germany entered the Soviet Union. Believing in their own superiority and the belief that 'The entire rotten edifice would collapse on its own', the largest military operation in history commenced. Thanks to a range of factors, where the placement of the Soviet troops right at the border was most essential, Nazi-Germany almost succeeded. Millions of Soviet soldiers were defeated, and colossal amounts of materials were destroyed and seized. The Red Army stumbled. However, the loss of time, the swaying German course, the logistical problems, the enormous extent of the country, the obstinacy of the climate and population, and the ruthless attitude of the Kremlin with terror and evacuation, resulted into less room for Von Bock at the gates of Moscow to carry out one last finale push. After countless campaigns of only six weeks, the Wehrmacht was now facing a war of exhaustion. From day one Moscow went to extremes. Nazi Germany still lived on guns and butter. Germany, which lacked raw materials, would, from December 1941, be at war with practically the entire world, and would lose more initiative year after year, until they perished in 1945. The basis for this downfall was made in 1941, where October 1941, would become the most important month, when, after months of doubts the final course was determined, with fatal consequences for Berlin.

Annex 1

The provided German Occupancy Forces Soviet Union after Capitulation

12 panzer divisions
6 motorized divisions
34 infantry divisions
3 mountain divisions
1 cavalry division
Total: 56 divisions

(Source KTB OKW Vortragnotiz 72 d. 15 July, 1941)

Soviet soldiers raise the red hammer and sickle over the Reichstag in Berlin on 2 May, 1945, after eventually defeating the Nazis.

Literature

Boog/Förster/Hoffmann/Klink/Müller/Ueberschar, der Angriff auf die Sowjetunion (Frankfurt am Main 1991)

Broekmeyer, M., Stalin de Russen en hun oorlog 1941-1945 (Amsterdam 1999)

Die Wehrmachtberichte 1939-1945. (band 1) (München 1985)

Dumans, V., De stalen vuist van de Blitzkrieg. De 1ste panzer Division 1939-1941 (Soesterberg 2013)

Glantz, D.M., The initial Period of War on the Eastern Front 22 June-August 1941 (London 1993)

Katamidze, S., de geheime diensten van de Sovjet-Unie. Van de Tsjeka tot de KGB. (2003)

Kreidler, E., Die Eisenbahnen im Zweiten Weltkrieg. Studien und Dokumente zur Geschichte des Zweiten Weltkrieges. (2001)

Kurowski, F., Balkenkreuz und Roter Stern. Der Luftkrieg über Russland 1941-1944

Lübbers,G.C., Wehrmacht und Wirstschaftsplanung für das Unternehmen 'Barbarossa'. Deutsche Ausbeutungspolitik in den besetzten Gebieten der Sowjetunion während des Zweiten Weltkrieges. (2010-Inaugural Dissertation)

Magenheimer,H., Militärstrategie Deutschlands 1940-1945. (München 2002)

Mallmann, K-M/Matthäus,J/Cüppers,M/Angrick,A. (hg.)., Deutsche Berichte aus dem Osten 1942/1943. Dokumente der Einsatzgruppen in der Sowjetunion Band III (Darmstadt 2014)

Messenger, C., Blitzkrieg. Eine Strategie macht Geschichte. (Augsburg 2000)

Militärgeograpischen Angaben über das Europäische Russland. Ukraine mit Moldaurepublik und Krim. Bildheft. (Sept. 1941)

Musial, B., Kampfplatz Deutschland. Stalins Kriegspläne gegen den Westen. (Berlin 2010)

Oetting, D.W., Verbrannte Erde. Kein Krieg wie im Westen: Wehrmacht und Sowjetarmee im Russlandkrieg 1941-1945. (Graz 2011)

Overy, R., Ruslands oorlog. (Soesterberg 2005)

Pierik, P., De geopolitiek van het Derde Rijk (Soesterberg 2013)

Literature

Pierik, P., Het onbekende Reich. Minder bekende feiten van het oostfront. (Soesterberg 2014)

Pierik, P., De zwarte magiër. Karl Haushofer, zijn invloed op Hitler en de kruistocht voor 'Lebensraum'. (Soesterberg 2015)

Pierik, P./Steeman, P., Stalingrad, de slag en de luchtbrug naar de dood. (Soesterberg 2014)

Rössler,M/Schleiermachrer, S., Der 'Generalplan Ost'. Hauptlinien der nationalsozialistischen Planung und vernichtungspolitik (Berlin 1993)

Russischer Kolonialismus in der Ukraine. Berichte und Dokumente (München 1962)

Schmidt, A., Ukraine. Land der Zukunft (Berlin 1939)

Schramm, P.E. (hg.). Kriegstagebuch des Oberkommandos der Wehrmacht 1940-1941 band I en band II (München 1982)

Senger und Etterlin, F.M.von., Die deutschen Panzer 1926-1945. (Bonn 1999)

Steiner,F., Von Clausewitz bis Bulganin. Erkenntnisse und Lehren einer Wehrepoche. (Bielefeld 1956)

Stupperich, R., Die Ukraine und das Baltenland. Tornister Schrift des Oberkommandos der Wehrmacht Abt. Inland. Heft 49.

Tessin, G., Verbände und Truppen der deutschen Wehrmacht und Waffen-SS im Zweiten Weltkrieg (Osnabrück 1975)

Urlanis, B.Z. Bilanz der krieg. Die Menschenverluste Europas vom 17.jahrhundert bis zur Gegenwart. (Berlin 1965)

Warlimont, W., Jim Hauptquartier der deutschen Wehrmacht 1939-1945. Grundlagen Formen, Gestalten. band I (1990)